STATHEAD SPORTS

STATHEAD
FOOTBALL

How Data Changed the Sport

by Michael Bradley

COMPASS POINT BOOKS

a capstone imprint

Stathead Sports is published
by Compass Point Books, a Capstone imprint
1710 Roe Crest Drive, North Mankato, Minnesota 56003
www.mycapstone.com

Library of Congress Cataloging-in-Publication Data
Names: Bradley, Michael J. (Michael John), 1956- author.
Title: Stathead football : how data changed the sport / by Michael Bradley.
Description: North Mankato, Minnesota : An imprint of Compass Point Books,
    published by Capstone, [2018] | Series: CPB Grades 4-8. Stathead sports |
    Audience: Ages: 9-14.
Identifiers: LCCN 2018021417 (print) | LCCN 2018032801 (ebook) | ISBN
    9781543514568 (eBook PDF) | ISBN 9781543514483 (hardcover) | ISBN
    9781543514520 (paperback)
Subjects: LCSH: Football¬—Statistics—Juvenile literature. |
    Football—Records—Juvenile literature.
Classification: LCC GV955 (ebook) | LCC GV955 .B73 2018 (print) | DDC
    796.332021—dc23
LC record available at https://lccn.loc.gov/2018021417

Editorial Credits
Nick Healy, editor; Terri Poburka, designer; Eric Gohl, media researcher;
Laura Manthe, production specialist

Photo Credits
AP Photo: 10; Dreamstime: Jerry Coli, 28, Michael Turner, 11; Getty Images:
Al Bello, 38, Bettmann, 12, Damian Strohmeyer, 41, Jamie Squire, 40, Jeff
Haynes, 37, Robert Beck, 29, Simon Bruty, 18; Newscom: Cal Sport Media/Jacob
Kupferman, cover, Icon Sportswire/Andrew Dieb, 4, Icon Sportswire/Rob Holt,
43, Icon Sportswire/David Rosenblum, 24, Icon Sportswire/Stephen Lew, 34,
TNS/Brian Peterson, 32, TNS/Max Faulkner, 6, UPI/Art Foxall, 44, UPI/Jim Bryant,
14, USA Today Sports/Chris Humphreys, 8, USA Today Sports/Erich Schlegel, 20,
USA Today Sports/Joe Nicholson, 15, USA Today Sports/Kelley L Cox, 17, USA
Today Sports/Mark Konezny, 26, USA Today Sports/Richard Mackson, 31, ZUMA
Press/Dan Anderson, 35; Shutterstock: Lightspring, back cover, 23

Design Elements: Shutterstock

Printed in the United States of America.
000964

TABLE OF CONTENTS

Game-Changing
DATA

▲ Wide receiver Alshon Jeffery of the Eagles celebrates after making a catch for a two-point conversion against the Cowboys.

When National Football League (NFL) coaches prepare for games, they make sure they have backups ready for action in case the starters get hurt. Most teams have three or four running backs ready to go. A collection of wide receivers prepares for work. Extra offensive linemen wait at the ready. And should the top two quarterbacks get hurt, someone on the team is designated the emergency signal-caller.

Coaches don't worry about suiting up a backup kicker because those guys don't usually get hurt.

Usually.

When the Philadelphia Eagles traveled to Dallas to face the Cowboys in November 2017, that way of doing things backfired. On the opening kickoff, the Eagles' placekicker Jake Elliott suffered a concussion while making a touchdown-saving tackle. He tried to kick later in the first quarter but missed a 34-yard field goal. Doctors ruled that he could not play again that night, and the Eagles were left with a problem.

The coaches had options such as using punter Donnie Jones as a substitute for Elliott on kickoffs, field goal attempts, and extra points. But Jones was the Eagles' holder, meaning head coach Doug Pederson would have unprepared subs holding and kicking. Pederson didn't want to risk that in such a big game. When the Eagles scored a touchdown, there was only one thing left to do—go for two.

Every time.

Philadelphia scored four touchdowns after Elliott left the game and were successful on three two-point tries. Some thought it was amazing. Others weren't so surprised.

According to the sports network ESPN, teams across the NFL have been successful on 47.9 percent of two-point attempts since 2001. And since 2013, the number of two-

▲ The Eagles sat kicker Jake Elliott after he missed a short field goal, and the team tried no field goals or extra points without him.

A big reason for the increase was the NFL's decision in 2015 to move the point-after kick from the 2-yard line to the 15-yard line. The league-wide success rate dropped on kicks for a point after touchdown (PAT). The rate of kicks made fell from above 97 percent to 94.4 percent. That means the expected value of the PAT is between 0.94 and 0.95 points (94.4 percent multiplied by 1 point).

Two-point attempts succeed less often but result in more points. Two-point tries have an expected value of 0.96 points (47.9 percent multiplied by 2 points). With those numbers in mind, going for two doesn't seem so risky anymore.

Clearly, NFL teams aren't going to go for two every time like the Eagles had to against Dallas. But the numbers show that it is a good bet. More than that, the recent increase in two-point tries shows that teams are more interested in advanced statistics than ever before. Teams used to pay attention only to the simple numbers, such as yards gained, passes caught, and field goals converted. Now they are diving deeper into data to gain edges over their rivals.

Coaches want to learn more about what makes players and teams successful. Teams are spending money to hire smart people to look at the numbers and find advantages. Franchises look at quarterbacks in terms of how well they pass on third down. Running backs need to pick up blitzing defenders, or they'll spend time on the bench. And defenders want data on how successful they are when rushing the passer or covering enemy receivers.

The basics of the NFL are the same: Touchdowns still count for six points, and field goals are worth three. But when it comes to the other numbers, teams are spending more time—and money—trying to get an advantage through stats. Advanced statistics have become vital in pro football.

CHAPTER 1

A TRADITION OF STATS

▲ Peyton Manning

Football is, above all, a team sport, but its most familiar statistics focus on the performance of individual players. For decades the pro football world has relied on stats that measure the success or failure of quarterbacks, receivers, running backs, and others. The sport's traditional stats help fans to assess star players—their successes and failures. These stats have been important for many years, and they continue to affect how fans watch and learn about football.

Peyton Manning was a superstar by many measures. Consider the numbers he racked up in 2013. Manning was amazing, even though he was 37 years old and only two years removed from missing a full season with a serious neck injury. He set a handful of NFL single-season records. They included: most passing yards (5,477), passing touchdowns (55), and pass attempts (659). His quarterback rating of 115.1 was the second highest he ever achieved. Many fans considered 2013 to be the greatest season of his Hall of Fame career.

Manning won the Most Valuable Player (MVP) award and led the Denver Broncos to the Super Bowl. Voters who named him MVP were no doubt impressed by his legendary numbers. They looked very good against the other top single-season passing performances in history.

Since the NFL began, players have been judged by simple totals—completions, yards gained, interceptions, etc. But a new collection of statistics is allowing fans to be more certain about who is the best of the best.

Traditional stats allowed the football world to see Manning as it had seen previous greats like Joe Montana, Fran Tarkenton, and Johnny Unitas. Running backs have been judged by the yards they gain since at least 1932. That was the first year the statistic was kept in the NFL. Boston Braves running back Cliff Battles led the league in rushing with 576 yards in 1932. (The Braves eventually became the Washington Redskins.) Running backs are also tracked by their yards per carry—an important statistic years ago and today.

Traditional stats showed the dominance of modern running back Adrian Peterson of the Minnesota Vikings. Just one season before Manning's big year, Peterson came within eight yards of history. He gained 2,097 yards on the ground. That put him in second place on the single-season rushing list, behind Eric Dickerson of the Los Angeles Rams. Dickerson's 2,105 yards in 1984 remains the NFL rushing record.

▶ Cliff Battles

Peterson's numbers in 2012 were impressive across the board. He scored 12 touchdowns in 2012 and averaged 6.0 yards per carry (yards gained divided by total carries). With the yardage from his 40 pass receptions, Peterson's season resulted in a league-leading 2,314 yards from scrimmage.

Old-school stats also show who stands out on the defensive side of the ball. Consider the case of Dick Lane. In 1952 he arrived in Los Angeles and asked for

▲ Adrian Peterson suffered a major knee injury late in the 2011 season but came back stronger in 2012.

a tryout with the Rams. He showed some good moves as a receiver and made the team, but the coaches soon moved him to the defensive backfield. It was a smart decision. In his rookie season, Lane set an NFL record with 14 interceptions while playing a 12-game schedule. He even returned two picks for touchdowns. (The NFL's regular season expanded to 14 games in 1961 and later to 16 games.)

▲ Dick Lane became known as "Night Train" because he enjoyed a hit song with that title.

Lane went on to intercept 68 passes during his career. When he retired, he ranked second in career interceptions. Paul Krause, who played for the Redskins and Vikings, later took the top spot on the list with 81 pick-offs. Lane is now fourth on the all-time list. His playing days ended more than 50 years ago, but today's defensive backs still measure themselves against him.

The interception remains the main statistic used to judge D-backs even though opposing teams often opt to avoid the NFL's most feared coverage men. In this case and others, the sport's most familiar stats simply don't tell the whole story.

In fact, more and more football insiders rely less and less on old-school ways of judging players and teams. Traditional stats provided the beginnings for new statistical tools that go deeper. Newer stats allow us to understand the game more completely. They help to show who is the most effective on the field and who does the most to help a team win. They help players, coaches, and fans better understand the game.

TOP RUSHERS

The all-time NFL leaders by average yards per carry.

RANK	NAME	TEAM	AVERAGE
1	Marion Motley	Browns	5.7
2	Jamaal Charles	Chiefs/Broncos	5.4
3	Jim Brown	Browns	5.2
4	Mercury Morris	Dolphins/Chargers	5.1
5 (tie)	Joe Perry	49ers/Colts	5.0
	Gale Sayers	Bears	5.0
	Barry Sanders	Lions	5.0

DON'T BE FOOLED

If Philadelphia fans looked only at the basic stats from the team's 24-10 loss to the Seattle Seahawks in December 2017, they might have thought Eagles quarterback Carson Wentz had a great game. They might have believed the second-year pro was amazing during the second half.

Wentz completed 29 of 45 passes (64.4 percent) for 348 yards and a touchdown. After intermission, he was particularly good, going 20-of-32 for 303 yards. The stats were another strong argument for his budding MVP hopes.

Sort of.

Sure, Wentz put up some big numbers. But the Eagles scored only 10 points. And in the second half, Wentz fumbled deep in Seahawks territory and threw an interception. He also tossed the ball over running back Kenjon Barner's head on a crucial fourth-and-three play, when Barner had plenty of open turf in front of him. And Wentz had Nelson Agholor open on a crossing pattern for what would have been a huge gain but underthrew the pass.

▲ Wentz coughed it up at the goal line.

In other words, while Wentz's raw numbers looked good, the stats were misleading. His team scored a mere 10 points. He committed two turnovers. He had the chance to create two big plays but didn't deliver. And his accuracy actually dropped in the second half—from 69.2 percent to 62.5 percent. His passer rating for the game, 86.2, was lower than his average rating of 102.0 rating at that point for the season.

There are lots of ways to make football statistics work for you. If you wanted to argue that Wentz played a good game, you could point to his 348 passing yards. That total looks pretty good. But it's not enough. Big numbers can fool some fans. It's important to understand that a big number isn't always as impressive as it looks.

Consider how coaches and fans judge running backs. It's tempting to measure them entirely on their total yards, but it might be more important to gauge their average yardage every time they touch the football. Look at the LeGarrette Blount results from 2016, when he was with the New England Patriots. Blount gained 1,161 yards that season but averaged only 3.88 per carry. Since the Pats had Tom Brady at quarterback, they didn't need a breakaway back. And Blount did score 18 touchdowns— mostly from short range—so in some ways he was effective for the Pats. But his low yardage per carry showed the limits of his play.

That season Frank Gore was also something of a curiosity. The Indianapolis Colts veteran gained 1,025

▲ LeGarrette Blount was a bulldozer in the backfield.

yards. Rushing for 1,000 yards has long been a mark of excellence in the NFL. By that standard, it would appear Gore had a successful season. But he averaged just 3.9 yards per carry, scored only four touchdowns, and averaged a modest 64 yards per game. The 1,000-yard standard doesn't mean what it once did. Gaining 1,000 yards when the NFL schedule was only 12 games long was impressive. Doing it in 14 games was a big deal too. With the 16-game schedule, reaching 1,000 yards says more about a back's good health and durability than his skills.

▲ DeAndre Hopkins makes a one-handed snag.

Wide receivers' numbers can be deceiving sometimes too. In 2016, Houston's DeAndre Hopkins caught 78 passes, a hefty number by any standard, especially since the Texans' quarterback situation wasn't so great. But Hopkins averaged only 12.2 yards per catch, not a great number for a top wideout. And he hauled in receptions only 51.7 percent of the time

QBs threw the ball his way. The low catch rate might be chalked up to the quarterbacks' inaccuracy. But Hopkins' catch rate was 7.1 percent lower than his number for 2015, when Houston's passers were no better. And his average yards per catch fell from season to season too. Hopkins is an outstanding receiver, but it's important to measure players completely. Don't be fooled by the numbers on their statistical line.

Defensive stats can be misleading too. Defensive backs are often judged by their interception totals. If a cornerback picks off six passes in a season, that looks great. But if three came in one game, the rest of the season wasn't so hot. And picks can be a factor of quarterbacks' inaccuracy, rather than a defender's ability to steal passes.

A better indicator is the opposing quarterbacks' completion percentages against an individual defensive back. The D-back probably isn't very strong if other teams are targeting receivers he is covering often and completing a high percentage of throws. That defender clearly isn't feared by opponents—even if he picks off six passes.

That's the way it goes with stats. They can be misleading, just as they can be useful. Fans should be careful not to be misled. It's important to look at the whole picture, and that requires diving deeper into the stat pool.

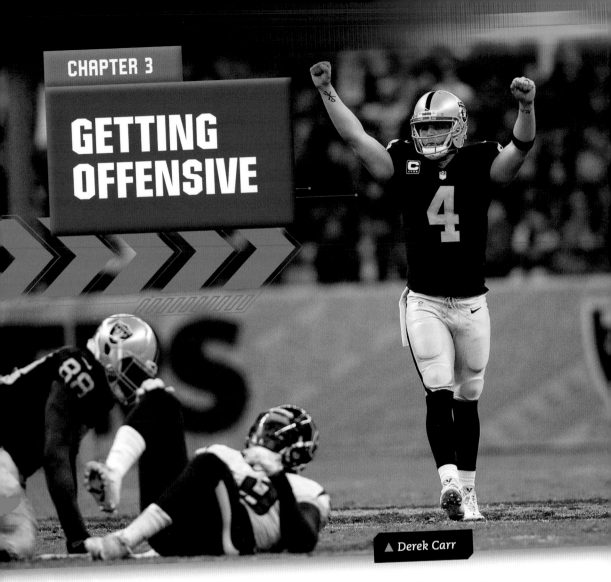

CHAPTER 3

GETTING OFFENSIVE

▲ Derek Carr

In 2016 the Oakland Raiders finally repaid their loyal and long-suffering fans for years of misery. After finishing at .500 or below for 13 consecutive seasons, the Raiders went 12-4 and reached the playoffs. They hadn't been in the postseason since 2002. Quarterback Derek Carr threw for 3,937 yards in just 15 games and earned his second Pro Bowl invitation. It was a great year, and many people expected even more success in 2017.

Not everyone was convinced, though. The Raiders outscored their opponents by a total of only 31 points in 2016. They were second in the AFC with 416 points but were far from a dominant team. They eked out a lot of close games. A statistic developed by Stats Inc. called the "Pythagorean expectation" predicted the Raiders would do worse 2017. The Stats Inc. team projected 8.7 wins for the Raiders in that season. Even that prediction proved too sunny. The Raiders won only six games, disappointing the team's "Black Hole" cheering section.

When it comes to offensive stats, it's not enough to look only at the pure numbers. It's important to dig deeper into things like point differentials, which can forecast future success or failure.

Teams that score a lot of points are usually able to generate big plays. They don't get their high totals only by grinding out clock-consuming, multi-play drives. Big plays are defined as runs of longer than 10 yards or pass plays longer than 25 yards. Seattle head coach Pete Carroll researched the impact of big plays. He found that more than 75 percent of drives that included at least one big play led to touchdowns or field goals. Drives without a big play were far less successful.

"Being able just to get one explosive play in a drive really increases your chances that you're going to score points," said Seahawks offensive coordinator Darrell Bevell.

He's right. Seattle finished in the top three in big play percentage (BPP) each season from 2012 through 2015. The team also made the playoffs every year. A team's BPP is found by dividing its total big plays by total plays. A good BPP is above 8 percent.

Quarterbacks who can produce big plays are in high demand, but there are plenty more ways to measure their effectiveness in today's NFL. One way is adjusted total QBR, an updated version of the NFL passer rating. Total QBR is a more complete look at quarterbacks. It takes into account performance on every play and measures passers' successes against good and poor defenses. For this new stat:

- Each QB "action play" (passes, rushes, sacks, scrambles, or penalties attributable to the QB) is measured in terms of the expected points added (EPA). This stat attempts to predict how many points will come on the current possession and future possessions.

- EPA is adjusted for the difficulty of each play. Adjustments are based on the type and depth of a pass and whether the QB was pressured.

- If there is a completion, the quarterback is credited only for the typical amount of yards after the catch based on the type and depth of the pass.

- There is a discount on trash time stats. Trash time occurs when the outcome of a game is certain near the end of a game—and defenses play soft so big offensive stats come easy.

- More credit is given when a quarterback is facing a tough defense—and vice versa.

- Total QBR averages the adjusted EPA per play and transforms it to a 0 to 100 scale, with 50 being average.

Total QBR goes beyond the individual quarterback stats. It looks at the type of defenses passers face and the degree of difficulty for each play. It also aims to find out how responsible a QB is for each play's success. A long completion in which the ball travels 50 yards in the air boosts the quarterback's Total QBR. On the other hand, the QB doesn't get much reward for throwing a screen pass that the receiver turns into a 50-yard gain.

In the 2017 regular season, Carson Wentz of the Eagles and Case Keenum of the Vikings sat atop the NFL in terms of Total QBR. Wentz's rating was 75.7, while Keenum's was 69.5. Perhaps not surprisingly, their teams met in the NFC Championship Game, although Wentz had been lost to an injury late in the regular season. At the bottom of the 2017 list were Mitchell Trubisky of the Bears (29.1) and Trevor Siemian of the Broncos (27.6).

Another way to judge a quarterback's performance is his completion percentage on third down. Most teams throw on third down, particularly if they have a long way

▲ Aaron Rodgers

to go to gain a first down. Before he tore his anterior cruciate ligament (ACL) in the Eagles' 13th game of the 2017 season, Wentz had completed 49.2 percent of his third-down throws. That's a high percentage, given how hard it is to be successful on third down. In 2017 fewer than half the teams converted third-down opportunities even 40 percent of the time.

Quarterbacks are also judged by how successful they are throwing different types of passes. In 2016 the New Orleans Saints' Drew Brees was the best in the NFL on screen passes, completing 67 of 70 attempts. The Green Bay Packers' Aaron Rodgers was the top man throwing passes 0 to 8 yards (84.8 percent completion rate), while Tom Brady of the Pats was the best at intermediate passes (9 to 18 yards), and Atlanta's Matt Ryan was the best deep ball thrower. Three of those four—Rodgers, Brady, and Ryan—have won MVP awards. And Brees is the active leader in career passing yards.

There are other ways to measure quarterback success. Adjusted completion percentage doesn't include drops, throwaways, batted passes, or throws in which the quarterback was hit. In 2016 the Vikings' Sam Bradford

led the NFL with an 80.9 percent adjusted rate. The Packers'
Rodgers had the best passer rating when getting hit, and
Dallas Cowboys rookie Dak Prescott was the most accurate
quarterback on play-action throws (passes that come after
faking a handoff to the running back).

New offensive stats can also predict how well running
backs will perform in certain situations. For example, it's
possible to measure which backs are best at specific down-
and-distance combinations (such as first-and-10 or third-
and-one). Stats also measure which back is the best at
gaining enough yards to get his team a first down. In 2016
Mike Gillislee, then with the Buffalo Bills, registered first
downs on 38.6 percent of his 101 attempts—best in the NFL.

TOP-RATED PASSERS

The 2017 leaders in the NFL by Total Quarterback Rating.

RANK	NAME	TEAM	RATING
1	Carson Wentz	Eagles	75.9
2	Case Keenum	Vikings	69.7
3	Tom Brady	Patriots	67.4
4	Dak Prescott	Cowboys	66.7
5	Matt Ryan	Falcons	63.7
6	Ben Roethlisberger	Steelers	63.2
7	Matthew Stafford	Lions	61.7
8	Alex Smith	Chiefs	61.6
9	Drew Brees	Saints	59.0
10	Russell Wilson	Seahawks	58.3

Three other important measurements are DYAR, DVOA, and success rate. Defense-adjusted yards above replacement (DYAR) shows how a runner compares, overall, to an average player at his position. Defense-adjusted value over average (DVOA) shows how a runner compares, per play, with an average RB. Rusher success rate aims to show which backs are most consistently successful.

Rushers with a high success rate can be relied on for production almost all of the time. They are not the sort of runners who get a few big plays that make their averages go up. If a running back gains two yards on a third-and-one, that hurts his per-carry average. But it was still a successful play because he earned his team a first down.

▲ Dion Lewis

In the 2017 NFL season, New England's Dion Lewis was first in DYAR, second in DVOA, and fourth in success rate. That's a pretty good performance level. The Rams' Todd Gurley and Saints' Alvin Kamara also ranked high on all three lists. Meanwhile, some well-known backs looked less impressive by these measurements. For example, Leonard Fournette of the Jaguars had a 44 percent success rate. That was only 26th in the league. He looked better—11th in the NFL—when judged by his DYAR, and he was 17th in DVOA.

New stats also provide a more careful look at receivers. Catch rate shows the percentage of passes thrown their way that they bring in. A receiver's catch rate is calculated by dividing his completions by the number of passes thrown to him. In 2016 the Saints' Michael Thomas had a 76.0 catch rate, tops among receivers with at least 50 targets.

That does not mean Thomas dropped the other 24 percent. No stat clearly shows why those passes were incomplete. They might have been dropped or knocked away by a defender. They might have fallen incomplete for other reasons. The value of the catch rate is that it shows what a player does when given a chance. Thomas ranked ninth in total catches that season. But his catch rate was much higher than the New York Giants' Odell Beckham's 59.8 percent, and Beckham is famous for his great hands. Meanwhile, the Arizona Cardinals' Larry Fitzgerald led the league with 107 catches. He had a catch rate of 71.3 percent.

2017 CATCH RATE LEADERS

RANK	NAME	TEAM	CATCHES	CATCH RATE
1	Ben Watson	Ravens	61	77.2%
2	Golden Tate	Lions	92	76.7%
3	Ted Ginn	Saints	53	75.7%
4	Austin Hooper	Falcons	49	75.4%
5	Jack Doyle	Colts	80	74.1%

CHAPTER 4

FOR THE DEFENSE

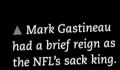

▲ Mark Gastineau had a brief reign as the NFL's sack king.

▲ Von Miller

Most fans know an old saying about football—the best offense is a good defense. There is, of course, truth in that nugget. Defense is vital to winning, and NFL defenses are judged ultimately on how many points they allow every game. It's nice to limit opponents from piling up yards, but it's possible to do fairly well by that measure and still give up a lot of points. Putting together a stingy defense requires coaches to look at a lot of new statistics.

It seems obvious that NFL quarterbacks do worse when they face more pass-rush pressure. That's why teams spend so much money on pass rushers. If you keep the opposing QB from feeling comfortable, he's unlikely to tear through the secondary.

That's why the NFL has celebrated the sack for years. So have the players. In the 1980s, New York Jets defensive end Mark Gastineau used to dance like someone had put a hot coal down his pants after he sacked the QB. These days, Denver's Von Miller has shown some fine dance moves after he brings down a quarterback behind the line.

But there's more to the story. While sacks are important and can be game changing, defensive linemen are judged by how they disrupt the offense overall. Pro Football Focus has come up with a statistic called pass rushing productivity (PRP). The stat measures a defensive lineman's overall ability to create havoc for the opposing team.

This stat comes with a complicated formula. Here's how it is measured: Add total sacks to the number of hits on the quarterback (multiplied by .75); add in the number of quarterback hurries (multiplied by .75) and divide by the number of times a lineman rushes the passer (multiplied by 100). A "quarterback hurry" comes when a defensive player forces the QB to throw the ball earlier than he wants to. A PRP score between 10 and 15 is considered outstanding. The goal is to show which players are the most disruptive to opposing pass offenses.

Complex statistics like pass rushing productivity decide how best to use players. For example, a defensive lineman who is successful rushing the passer but not stopping the run would be used more in passing situations. That means the player would likely shuttle in for second down or third down. Or perhaps the team has a linebacker who excels against the run but not the pass. Coaches will replace that player in likely passing situations. The goal is to find the best ways to deploy talent at the right times.

▶ Bobby Wagner wraps up a runner.

The 2017 Seahawks relied on linebacker Bobby Wagner, thanks to his all-around talent. Wagner is an outstanding tackler whose efficiency rating (how often a player makes a tackle when he has the chance) is very high. He also has a high run-stop percentage (number of tackles made on all running plays against a defense).

Wagner can play good pass defense too. But he wasn't in the same class as the Eagles' linebacker Jordan Hicks. When Hicks tore his Achilles tendon in late October of 2017, the Eagles lost the league's top linebacker against the pass. Opposing QBs had a meager 53.7 passer rating when throwing in his direction in 2016, a number that was 23.1 points better than the next finisher. That's a pretty impressive performance.

▲ Xavier Rhodes has made his name as a shutdown corner.

Like the sack, the interception is a dramatic, game-changing play. Often defensive backs have been judged by their ability to register interceptions. But they are now measured more closely as teams try to figure out who is least successful against the pass.

For some reason, opposing coaches at one time thought that person was Jacksonville's Jalen Ramsey. The Jaguars' cornerback was the most targeted DB in the NFL during the last five weeks of the 2016 season. It was curious that this happened because Ramsey allowed rival QBs to register only a 37.8 rating. Furthermore, he amassed 11 combined interceptions and pass breakups while allowing receivers to catch just 17 passes. It was an amazing performance by Ramsey. He let the rest of the NFL know just how bad an idea it was to go after him.

Minnesota cornerback Xavier Rhodes didn't have a stretch that rivaled Ramsey's, but his season overall was better. Rhodes led all cornerbacks with a 47.0 passer rating allowed. Rhodes was a big reason the 2016 Vikings' defense finished third in the league in passing yards allowed and fourth in opposing passer rating.

Rhodes' results provide another example of how a closer look at the numbers can reveal things about players and teams that ordinary statistics don't.

THE NFL'S STINGIEST DEFENSES

Good defenses might stop other teams from gaining a lot of yards, but the real test of a D is how many points it allows. Here are the teams that have limited opponents to the fewest per game in a season.

RANK	TEAM	YEAR	POINTS PER GAME
1	Falcons	1977	9.2
2	Vikings	1969	9.5
3	Rams	1975	9.6
4 (tie)	Steelers	1975	9.9
	Vikings	1971	9.9

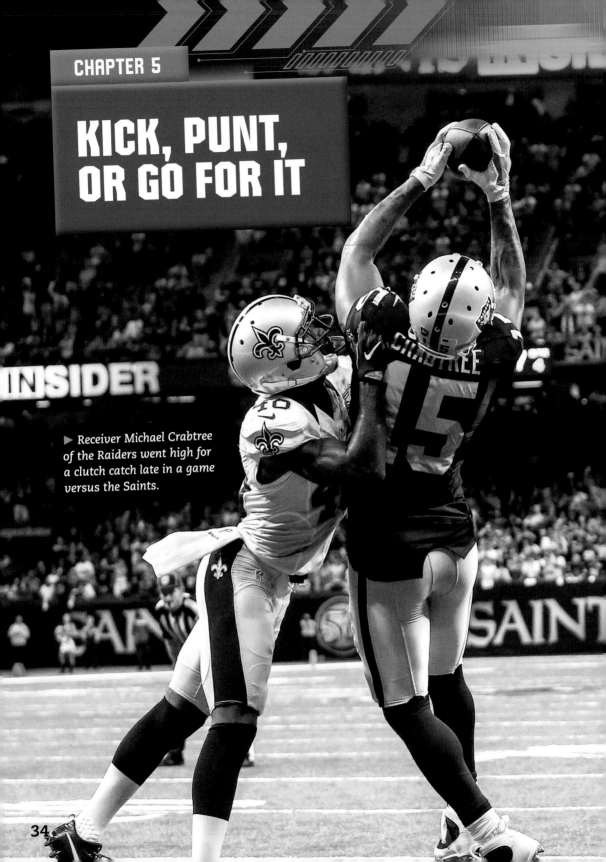

CHAPTER 5

KICK, PUNT, OR GO FOR IT

▶ Receiver Michael Crabtree
of the Raiders went high for
a clutch catch late in a game
versus the Saints.

In the second half of the 2016 season opener, the Raiders found themselves down 14 points to the host Saints. It's never easy to beat the Saints in the Superdome. Spotting them a two-TD lead makes things even tougher.

But there was Raiders quarterback Derek Carr, leading a comeback. Carr hit Seth Roberts with a 10-yard TD pass with only 47 seconds remaining to make the score 34-33. The Saints still had a one-point lead. If the Raiders converted the point-after touchdown kick, the game probably would've gone to overtime. Anything can happen in overtime.

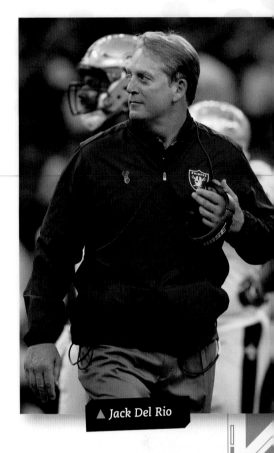

▲ Jack Del Rio

Raiders coach Jack Del Rio wasn't in the mood for extra football. He kept his offense on the field and instructed it to try for two points. After the game, he explained his reasoning quite simply.

"We're here to win," he said. "Let's win it right now."

Carr threw a fade into the left corner of the end zone, and receiver Michael Crabtree went up over a defender

and grabbed it. Two points. Oakland took the lead, 35-34, and held on as time ran out on the Saints. Maybe Del Rio's big decision was influenced by a fear of Saints quarterback Drew Brees. The passing legend had already thrown for 392 yards and would be dangerous in overtime. Or maybe Del Rio was playing a hunch.

Perhaps there was another explanation for Del Rio's call. In going for two, he would be joining the growing number of NFL coaches who have decided it makes sense to go for two more often. The number of two-point conversion tries has climbed in recent years.

The NFL made the PAT kick longer—and therefore less successful—in 2015. That change has a big impact on teams' decisions. Coaches know there's a nearly 50 percent chance their team will get the two-point conversion. Before the rule change, kickers made more than 97 percent of extra points. In the first season after the change, they made 94.2 percent. That's still a very high number, but it's not the lock it seemed to be before.

So coaches are going for two more often. They do it in key situations like Oakland's late-game chance. They also do it when a two-point conversion can push a lead to nine points, meaning their opponent must score at least twice to take the lead.

Teams try to make the choice easier by relying on data. A chart developed by former Eagles, Rams, and Chiefs coach Dick Vermeil remains a guide for many coaches. It

▲ Dick Vermeil became a coaching legend.

outlines what to do in situations when a team leads or trails by a certain amount of points late in a game. For instance, if a team scores a TD to go up one point, it should go for two. That way a last-second field goal by the opponent will tie the game, rather than giving that squad a one-point win. If a team scores to shrink a deficit to five, it should go for two—to narrow the gap to three. That way, a field goal could tie it.

A similar blend of math and guts has been applied to the decision about when to go for it on fourth down. For decades, it was rare to see a team try a fourth-down conversion, especially in its own territory. When fourth down came, the punter ran onto the field. That was it. Now many more teams are going for it.

Why? Because it works.

NFL teams succeeded on 51.41 percent of fourth-down tries in 2016, up 8.05 percent from 2011. Thirteen teams converted more than 50 percent of the time. Eight of those teams made first downs more than 60 percent of the time. The Eagles had the most attempts (27) but finished 17th in the league in success rate with a 48.1 percent mark.

▲ A pass sailed past Jordan Matthews on one of the Eagles' failed two-point attempts in a loss to the Giants.

Teams don't often try it deep in their own territory unless it's late in the game and they are desperate. It doesn't make much sense to take a chance of giving the other team a short distance to travel for points. Once offenses reach midfield and beyond, the thinking changes. A fourth-down try risks less.

Fans love it when teams go for it on fourth down. But the Eagles found out how tough things can be if you don't succeed. In 2016 against the Giants, they went for it on fourth down twice deep in New York territory. The Eagles passed up what would have been easy field goal tries. They failed both times. After the Eagles lost, 28-23, plenty of people wished they had kicked the field goals rather than trying to get more.

"It shows confidence and belief in the guys," Eagles coach Doug Pederson said after the game. "At that time, I felt like we were moving the ball."

In another 2016 game, Houston trailed Oakland, 27-20, with 3:13 to go and only one time out remaining. Facing a fourth-and-five from the Texans' own 44, coach Bill O'Brien decided to punt. The Texans never got the ball back. Afterward O'Brien was apologetic.

"If I had it back, I'd go for it," he said.

By doing so, he would've joined a growing group of fellow coaches who want to take some chances.

HISTORY OF THE TWO-POINT CONVERSION

The two-point conversion is not an NFL invention. It was first used in college football in 1958. That year, teams actually attempted more two-point tries than point-after kicks (1,371-1,295 in 578 games). The Canadian Football League adopted it in 1975.

The NFL brought in the rule in 1994. The first successful conversion came when Cleveland punter and kick holder Tom Tupa scored on a fake PAT against Cincinnati in the first week of the season. Tupa scored on two other fakes that season, earning him the nickname "Two-Point Tupa."

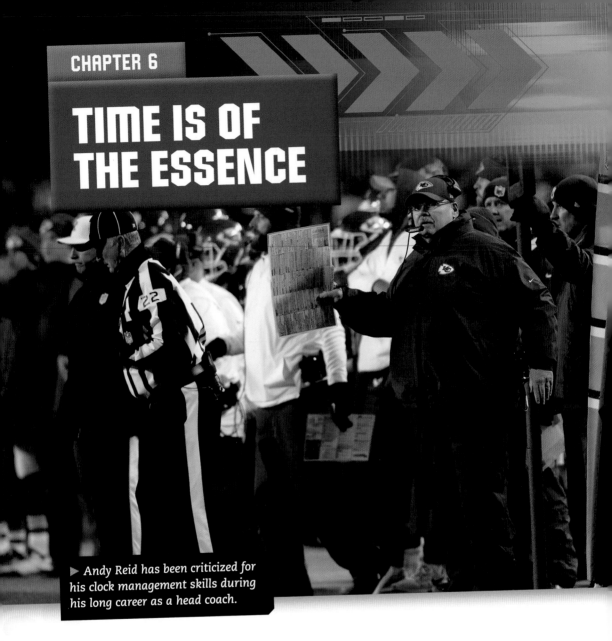

CHAPTER 6

TIME IS OF THE ESSENCE

▶ Andy Reid has been criticized for his clock management skills during his long career as a head coach.

Kansas City coach Andy Reid wasn't too interested in talking about his clock management work at the end of the Chiefs' 18-16 playoff loss to Pittsburgh in January 2017.

"I'm not sure exactly what you're talking about," he said to a reporter after the game.

That seemed strange to a lot of people. Many others were discussing how Reid struggled again to make the most of the 60 minutes available in an NFL game. It brought back memories of Super Bowl XXXIX. Reid was coaching the Eagles, who were down 10 to New England with 5:40 left in the fourth quarter. Rather than play fast, Philadelphia took its time on a scoring drive and didn't have time to make a complete comeback. The Patriots won, 24-21.

Against the Steelers, the Chiefs were behind, 18-10, when they took over on their own 25. They scored a touchdown, but it took 7:06 to get there. Their two-point conversion failed because of a holding call, so the Chiefs still trailed, 18-16. Pittsburgh then ran out the remaining 2:43 of the clock to win the game.

▼ The Patriots close in on QB Donovan McNabb in their 2005 Super Bowl win over the Eagles.

A year earlier, the Chiefs trailed the Patriots in the playoffs, 27-13, with 6:29 left and needed two touchdowns to tie. Instead of playing quickly, the Chiefs moved like time wasn't an issue. They scored a touchdown, but only 1:13 remained. The only option left was an onside kick, which didn't work. Reid's team lost, 27-20.

Every Sunday coaches face decisions about how to manage the clock. It could be at the end of the first half or late in the fourth quarter, when decisions have to be made about when to speed things up and when to slow them down. Games are won and lost sometimes based on whether teams create enough time for a comeback or drain enough time to preserve a lead.

It's not easy to manage the clock properly. No two games are the same. So much happens on the field during a game that it is tough to get things right in the middle of the first quarter. When time is running out and a team is trying to figure out what it must do to win a game, it gets even more complicated.

One NFL assistant coach described it this way: "The closest comparison we could come up with was an air traffic controller. You've got a thousand things going on, you're watching 20 planes…"

Perhaps it's not that dangerous. But it can be confusing. Miami head coach Adam Gase says the unpredictable nature of the game makes things especially hard. No one knows what will happen from one play to another. And with under a minute to make decisions about whether to call a time-out and what play to run, it can get kind of crazy.

In 2015 a record 131 NFL games were decided by seven or fewer points. Clock management was a factor in most of them. The same day Reid's Chiefs ran out of time against New England, Arizona Cardinals coach Bruce Arians also made some poor decisions.

His Cardinals led Green Bay, 17-13, with 2:34 left. They had a second down on Green Bay's 22. They might have gone for a touchdown. Or they could have taken their time, drained the clock, and kicked a field goal to win. But Arians called for a pass on second down. It went incomplete, and the clock stopped. Arizona couldn't make a first down, so it settled for a field goal that made it 20-13 with 1:55 left. Aaron Rodgers led the Packers on a long drive to tie the game at the end of regulation, thanks to the extra time that incompletion gave him.

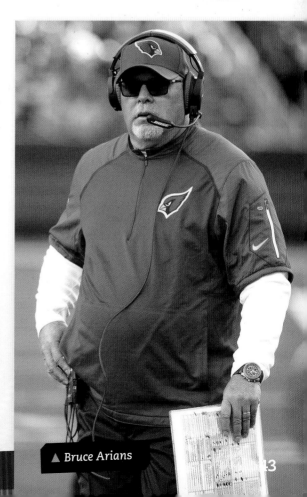

▲ Bruce Arians

The good news for Arizona? Carson Palmer led the team to victory in overtime. But the extra tension might not have been necessary if Arians' decision hadn't left Green Bay with so much extra time.

There is no set formula for good clock management. It takes experience and quick decision-making. Coaches have assistants to help manage the clock at the end of halves and games. They need advice from people who can look two or three plays ahead. And they must be clear in what they want to do. It sure isn't easy.

▲ Larry Fitzgerald

"You can prepare yourself," says Darren Rizzi, the Dolphins' assistant who helps head coach Adam Gase with clock-related decisions, "but the unpredictability is why I don't think anyone can ever truly master it. Even the best coaches have made mistakes."

And they will likely make them again.

WALK-OFF PUNT RETURN

In 2010, Kevin Boss caught an eight-yard TD pass from Eli Manning with 8:17 left in the fourth quarter to give the Giants a 31-10 lead over Philadelphia. It looked like New York would push its record to 10-3 on the season.

But the Eagles fought back. The score was 31-31 when Philly's DeSean Jackson prepared to catch Matt Dodge's punt with 14 seconds to play. Dodge's kick was a line drive, and Jackson took it on the Philadelphia 35, backpedaled to the 30, and headed upfield. He broke through a group of Giants tacklers at the 45 and got a huge block from teammate Jason Avant at midfield.

Jackson ran untouched to the goal line. But not wanting to leave time for the Giants to receive a kickoff, he did not step into the end zone until the clock hit 0:00. It was the perfect blend of a great play and excellent clock management. And it gave the Eagles a big victory.

STAT GLOSSARY

adjusted completion percentage—a quarterback's success rate when dropped passes, deflected throws, and throw-aways are not counted

adjusted total QB rating—a statistic created to provide a complete look at a quarterback's success based on a formula that includes the difficulty of each play, quality of opponents, and garbage-time stats

big play percentage—calculated by dividing the total number of big plays by the amount of plays a team runs over 16 games; big plays are running plays of 10 or more yards and passing plays of 25 or more yards

defensive efficiency rating—how often a player makes a tackle when he has a chance; calculated by dividing total tackles by opportunities

fourth-down success rate—how often a team converts fourth down tries; calculated by dividing successful attempts by total attempts

opposing passer rating—success rate of opposing QBs against individual linebackers and defensive backs

passer rating—a complicated formula that attempts to measure a quarterback's ability based on a variety of factors including completion percentage, number of touchdown passes versus interceptions, and yards per pass attempted

pass rushing productivity—effectiveness of a defender based on the number of sacks, QB hits, and QB hurries he achieves on plays when he rushes the passer

point after touchdown success rate—how often kickers and teams are able to convert point-after tries following TDs

Pythagorean expectation—a calculation, based primarily on a team's average margin of victory from the previous season, that forecasts how many games the team will win the next season

target percentage—how often a receiver catches passes for which he's the target; calculated by dividing receptions by passes to him

touchdowns per target—rate at which players score TDs when quarterbacks throw the ball to them; calculated by dividing a player's receiving touchdowns by the total number of times he is targeted with a pass

two-point success rate—rate at which teams are able to convert their two-point attempts after touchdowns

READ MORE

Doeden, Matt. *Fantasy Football Math: Using Stats to Score Big in Your League*. North Mankato, Minn.: Capstone Press, 2017.

Gramling, Gary, and The Editors of Sports Illustrated Kids. *The Football Fanbook: Everything You Need to Become a Gridiron Know-it-All*. New York: Sports Illustrated Kids, 2017.

Savage, Jeff. *Football Super Stats*. Minneapolis: Lerner Publications, 2018.

INTERNET SITES

Use FactHound to find Internet sites related to this book.

Visit **www.facthound.com** Just type in 9781543514483 and go.

Super-cool stuff! Check out projects, games and lots more at **www.capstonekids.com**

INDEX